DRUG ABUSE RELAPSE
HELPING TEENS TO GET CLEAN AGAIN

Students gather for a SADD demonstration in Washington, DC.

DRUG ABUSE RELAPSE
HELPING TEENS TO GET CLEAN AGAIN

Barbara Moe

The Rosen Publishing Group, Inc.
New York

Published in 2000 by The Rosen Publishing Group, Inc.
29 East 21st Street, New York, NY 10010

Library of Congress Cataloging-in-Publication Data

Moe, Barbara A.
   Drug abuse relapse : helping teens to get clean again / Barbara Moe.
      p. cm. — (The drug abuse prevention library)
   Includes bibliographical references and index.
   Summary: Discusses the problem of falling back into drug abuse, what causes relapses, and how to get help in breaking the cycle of continued drug dependence.
   ISBN 0-8239-3157-9 (lib. bdg.)
   1. Teenagers—Drug use—United States—Juvenile literature. 2. Teenagers—Counseling of—United States—Juvenile literature. 3. Narcotic habit—Relapse—United States—Juvenile literature. [1. Drug abuse.] I. Title. II. Series.
HV5824.Y68M62 2000
362.29'18'0835—dc21
                       99-049333

Contents

Teens who have a drug-use relapse often find themselves out of control.

Introduction

One summer Matt "borrowed" his dad's car and crashed it. He was only fifteen years old. Matt lost control of the car and it spun into a cornfield. Luckily no injuries resulted, except to the corn. Matt himself was so stoned that he did not remember taking the car, much less crashing it. The accident scared his dad, who got Matt into a residential treatment center from which he graduated. But after making a fresh start in another new school that fall, Matt began using drugs again. He experienced a relapse.

Relapse means going back to using drugs or alcohol after a period of not using them. No matter how long a former drug user has been abstinent (a nonuser), relapse is always a possibility. From the minute a person attempts recovery, he or

8 | she should make a plan for what to do in case of relapse, or in case the warning signs of relapse appear.

This book will help you to understand the process of addiction—how it happens and how it affects a person's life. You will also learn about the process of recovery and how to get there. Recovery means abstaining from the use of drugs and alcohol. We'll take a look at the role of emotions such as anger, fear, sadness, guilt, and loneliness and how they affect both addiction and recovery. Those in recovery learn to make positive changes in themselves and in their lifestyles. Armed with self-knowledge and the help of family, friends, counselors, and support groups, these people work at becoming stronger than ever before.

Not all people in recovery have relapses, but many do. This book will give you tips on relapse prevention, including a description of the warning signs of relapse, how to avoid putting yourself in high-risk situations, how to lead a happy and balanced life while staying drug- and alcohol-free, and how to make use of the help that is out there.

If you do relapse, all is not lost. You will learn how to give yourself a break, pick yourself up, dust yourself off, and try again.

CHAPTER 1

What Is Addiction?

Matt did not have many friends, but the ones he did have called him a man of few words. He was clumsy and not very good at sports. In fact, Matt couldn't think of many things he was good at. He could smoke pot, though, and he could drink a lot of beer. Both lifted his spirits—at least for a while. When the effects of the substances wore off, however, Matt felt bad about himself and needed more drugs and alcohol. When his parents divorced, Matt had to move back and forth between Minnesota and Iowa. He felt like a homeless person. To forget his troubles, Matt drank more beer and smoked more pot.

Almost any substance or almost any activity that human beings are involved in

Drug addiction is a pattern of behavior in which a person has a compulsion to use illegal, mind-altering substances.

can become addictive. This book will focus on how to keep from relapsing into negative addictions, specifically those involving drugs and alcohol. Drug addiction is a pattern of behavior in which a person has a compulsion to use illegal, mind-altering substances in spite of their adverse effects. With severe drug addiction, the person values the use of that substance more than anything else.

Kate looks forward to a big bowl of popcorn every night. She says that she is "addicted" to popcorn. Ben has a soda every day with lunch. But Ben can substitute juice or water for his lunchtime soft drink, and

Kate does not suffer from withdrawal symptoms if she runs out of popcorn.

Kate and Ben are not suffering from the disruptive effects that chemical substances can have on people's lives. They are not really addicted. Addictive behaviors are overwhelming urges and intense cravings. Addiction to drugs causes problems in the lives of addicted persons and those close to them. Addictive behaviors can ruin lives and can kill the addicted person or others. The high a person gets from using drugs is followed by a low that may include physical discomfort or intense pain, depression and low self-esteem, and loss of control—hardly problems for the popcorn or soda "addict."

Ways of Looking at Addiction

Most experts in relapse prevention use three different models to describe addiction: the moral model, the disease model, and the addictive-behavior model. Those who subscribe to the moral model consider addiction a failure of willpower or a lapse in character. The disease model, sometimes called the medical model, looks at hereditary influences as some of the possible underlying causes of addiction and

12 | considers people powerless to cope with their addictions. A third approach, the addictive-behavior model, regards substance abuse and problem drinking as very powerful bad habits. Proponents of this model believe that a person who has learned addictive behaviors can unlearn them.

Though moral persuasion is certainly part of drug counseling, most professionals in this field are uncomfortable with the moral model because it tends to make severe judgments of people's characters. Telling an addict that he or she is a bad person is not an effective way to encourage a change in behavior. The disease model has some validity because hereditary factors do play a role in certain addictive behaviors, but regarding people as powerless to control their addictions leaves therapists few options. The addictive-behavior model, on the other hand, implies that bad habits can be changed through a variety of counseling techniques.

How Addiction Develops

Five high school girls have a wine-drinking party at Sara's house while her parents are out. Bob and Jack share a joint behind the restaurant where they work as dishwashers. Carol steals some of her mom's prescription

diet pills to give her a high so that she can **13**
study all night. Ron works on set design at
summer camp, and someone offers him a few
lines of cocaine.

None of these young people plan to become addicted, and maybe none will. However, all are now at risk for developing a substance abuse disorder. Experimentation with alcohol or drugs is the first step toward addiction. If addiction progresses to its second stage, the person begins to need chemical substances to relax and have fun.

Jack began to believe that he could face the greasy water and heat of the dish room only if he got a little stoned. Pot seemed like a relatively inexpensive answer to his problems.

In the third stage of addiction, drug use becomes the focal point of people's lives. They may start using other drugs, they may drop friends who do not use in favor of drug-using friends, they may stop doing homework or drop out of school, or they may stop caring about their appearance. They may even steal to get enough money to support their drug habit. Increasingly, they will need more and more drugs to

14 | produce the original effects, since continued use has now dulled the high.

Jack started conducting drug deals at his "office" by the back door of the restaurant. Not only did he start skipping classes, but he slacked off at work. One night the boss sent his college-age son to the back door to buy some dope from Jack. The police were right behind him.

The final stage of drug addiction occurs when the person has to use the drug in order to feel normal. At this stage, drug use is not fun anymore; it's misery. The drug has made the user dependent on higher and higher doses.

Buying and using drugs is dangerous and illegal.

CHAPTER 2

The Effects of Drugs and Alcohol

Drugs and alcohol affect many aspects of people's lives, including their psychological (mental and emotional) processes and their physical condition.

Psychological Effects

The effects of drugs on a person's emotional life get more severe over time. Take fear, for example. The drug user fears getting caught, testing positive for drugs, getting kicked out of school or being fired from a job, not being able to find enough money to remain supplied with drugs, and being killed by drug dealers. Other feelings include anger and rage, shame, guilt, sadness, helplessness, and depression. Some people on drugs have suicidal or homicidal thoughts.

One trait that those who abuse drugs and alcohol often share is denial. Denial of the problem is one way people avoid dealing with guilt. That is why caring people such as therapists or relatives may organize an intervention. The goal of an intervention is to confront the addicted person with the behaviors that have hurt him or her or others and to get the person to admit to the problem and to get help for the addiction. Once people break through their denial and admit that they have a problem, they are taking the first step toward recovery.

During her first year of high school, Sara started drinking and occasionally used drugs. A shy girl, she liked getting buzzed, which made her feel brave and funny. By the time Sara was a junior, she believed that she couldn't do anything social unless she had had something to drink. Before her prom, she got into her dad's supply of liquor. Before she had even arrived at the dance, Sara got sick all over her date's tuxedo and he had to take her home. The next day, Sara decided to get help.

One result of the use of drugs as a way of coping with stress is that the person loses the opportunity to solve problems and grow into a mature person. After

Addicted people often try to hide their destructive behavior from friends and family.

"detox" and in recovery, that person will have a lot of catching up to do.

Physical Effects

The physical effects of drugs vary depending on the drug used. However, almost any drug in high doses (acute use) or over time (chronic use) can kill. The physical effects are most obvious during intoxication and withdrawal. The following are some of the most commonly abused drugs and their physical effects.

Alcohol (ethanol) is a drug teens abuse often. Many young people believe that alcohol makes them lively, stimulating companions. Actually, alcohol is a depressant. It results in impaired judgment, which can lead to car accidents, drownings, falls, suicides, and homicides. Heavy drinking can cause slurred speech, difficulty walking, coma, and death. Pregnant women who drink can cause serious birth defects in their babies.

Amphetamines include amphetamine (Benzedrine or "bennies"), dextroamphetamine (Dexadrine or "dex"), and methamphetamine (Methedrine, "meth," or "speed"). "Ice" is a very addictive methamphetamine that people smoke. "Crank" is the street name for another central nervous system stimulant in the amphetamine category. These drugs, also called uppers, are stimulants. They trigger the release of adrenaline and make a person feel excited, or "wired," restless, talkative, and irritable. They can play the cruel joke of making people think that they are performing exceptionally well when actually they are not. Doctors used to prescribe them for weight control.

Cocaine is similar in its effects to amphetamines, except for the length of the high. Cocaine's effects last for a much shorter time. Cocaine hydrochloride is a powder. People snort it or dissolve it in water and inject it. Cocaine freebase, or "crack," is usually smoked. Cocaine intoxication can make people confused, delirious, and paranoid. It can also make the heart stop.

Hallucinogens include LSD (lysergic acid diethylamide) and PCP (phencyclidine). LSD, or "acid," sometimes causes "bad trips" in which reality gets distorted and the person feels as if he or she is coming unglued. Even after a person stops using the drug, he or she can still have acid flashbacks. Veterinarians originally used PCP as an anesthetic. Some of its street names include "angel dust," "hog," "embalming fluid," and "rocket fuel." PCP can cause delusions and hallucinations as well as violent behavior.

Inhalants include paint thinners, model airplane glue, antiperspirants, nonstick vegetable sprays, fuels, and shoe polish. Inhalation of these substances causes a quick high in addition to possible nausea and vomiting. Other effects are confusion, impulsive behavior, trouble walking, seizures, and cardiac arrest.

Marijuana, or "pot," is usually smoked but can also be eaten. It can cause impairment of short-term memory, distortion of time, sluggishness, lack of motivation, feelings of panic, delusions, hallucinations, impairment of judgment, irritation of the respiratory tract, and bronchitis. The long-term health effects of marijuana are unknown because many people who smoke marijuana also smoke cigarettes.

Narcotics are also called opiate narcotics. Doctors prescribe drugs like morphine and codeine as painkillers. Not many teens abuse these drugs, but those who do suffer. Another narcotic, heroin, is usually injected, which puts the user at risk for HIV infection.

Sedative-hypnotics (sleeping pills) and **antianxiety medications** include barbiturates and benzodiazepines. Doctors prescribe the newer benzodiazepines for muscle strain, tension, sleep problems, and anxiety or panic attacks. Some of the common trade names are Ativan, Halcion, Klonopin, Librium, Restoril, Valium, and Xanax. Abuse of sedative-hypnotics can cause many of the symptoms of alcohol abuse. Combining these drugs with alcohol is especially dangerous and can kill. Sudden withdrawal can cause seizures and death.

CHAPTER 3

Recovery

The process of recovery usually takes place in three stages. In the first stage, a person decides to stop using drugs and makes a commitment to change. The second stage involves quitting alcohol or drug use and adjusting to living substance-free. The third stage is relapse prevention.

The Recovery Process

Recovery from drug dependence or substance abuse is a process that affects all aspects of a person's life. It changes that person's self-image and his or her relationships with friends and family.

In the winter after Matt's relapse, he lived with his mother in Minneapolis. At the apartment complex, he started talking to a girl named

Naomi who had similar problems. A few weeks   **23**
later, Naomi invited Matt to her therapy group.
During the first meeting, Matt felt a sense of
warmth, caring, and acceptance that he had
never experienced before. At the end of the
meeting, when he heard the words "Keep
coming back," Matt wanted to.

Recovery for Matt did not happen overnight,
but at school, he started hanging out with a dif-
ferent crowd instead of the "using" group. Matt
began to spend weekends on long bike rides with
Naomi and a couple of her friends from church.
Three years later, he's a drug- and alcohol-free
high school senior on his way to college.

We might say that Matt's story has a happy ending. When dealing with an addiction, however, there is no ending. The threat of relapse lurks in a corner, waiting for the person to let down his or her guard. A person should consider recovery from an addiction to be a lifelong process.

Getting Started

Getting drugs out of the body (detoxification) is the first step for anyone determined to stop abusing drugs. People with the most severe chemical dependency problems go to a hospital or residential treatment facility for "detox." Those who go

Recovery can take a long time, but the benefits are worth it.

this route will also have a period of inpatient rehab (rehabilitation) lasting up to a month. The third part of the program, aftercare, takes place after the person goes back home. Aftercare usually involves the former addict's attending a support group. People who can stop drug use on their own without experiencing withdrawal symptoms may use an outpatient clinic.

Recovery is much more than detoxification, however. It is a daily process that requires work on the part of the recovering person, who must make major life changes. A person cannot expect to stop the use of drugs and to make life changes without support. Would we expect people with asthma or diabetes to cure themselves?

Once a person has decided to get help and is actually getting it, he or she may at first feel a tremendous sense of relief. At last, the person thinks, the monkey is off his or her back. But when the reality of what he or she is attempting sinks in, this person may feel anxiety and an overwhelming sense of loneliness and loss.

As soon as he or she is drug-free, the person in a residential (live-in) program may participate in individual, group, or family therapy sessions; meditation training; education about substance abuse; and

26 | twelve-step programs such as Alcoholics Anonymous (AA), Narcotics Anonymous (NA), and Cocaine Anonymous (CA).

Becoming drug-free is only the beginning of many exciting life changes for those in recovery. Like everyone else in the world, the former addict attempts to find a life balance.

Finding a Life Balance

Who wants to be on top of the world? We all do. Working toward a balanced life is one of the best ways to get "high on life" and achieve control without the use of drugs and alcohol.

According to relapse prevention expert Alan G. Marlatt, a balanced life contains as many *wants* as *shoulds. Shoulds* are the things you have to do, such as going to school, doing homework, and cleaning your room. Examples of *wants* might include going to lunch with friends, taking a swim on a hot day, or staring at the stars on a clear night. A *should* for one person may be a *want* for another person. Try writing out your *wants* and *shoulds* and see if they balance. If they do, you are in good shape. If the *shoulds* outnumber the *wants,* you could be heading for a relapse. In order to keep your recovery on track, try to look at the following suggestions as your *wants.*

Taking Care of Your Body 27

Taking care of your body can become a major positive activity for the recovering addict. After all, it is the only body you have. You can begin by examining your eating habits and changing your diet, but don't expect to change your eating habits overnight. Healthy eating is one way of valuing yourself.

"Yesterday for lunch," says Megan, "I had a peach with some cottage cheese and a hunk of wheat bread. I compared how I felt that day with the day before, when I'd had two slices of double-cheese pizza. Ugh! After that pizza, my stomach rebelled. I think I'll try peaches more often."

Workouts

Physical exercise is another *should* that may in time evolve into a *want*. Does the prospect of an hour on the treadmill every day make you break into a cold sweat? Exercise does not have to take place indoors. You could choose a bike ride (instead of a car ride) to school or a walk in the park with a friend. Scheduling thirty minutes of some kind of exercise three times a week is enough for a start.

28

"During my drugging days," says Ashley, "my mom and I were at each other's throats constantly. If we weren't arguing, we were sulking and trying to get over it. As far back as I could remember, Mom had complained about being out of shape. When I started recovery, I suggested that we go swimming together a couple of times a week. I can't tell you how good that exercise and time together makes us both feel. It's great."

Sleep

In addition to exercise, get plenty of sleep. Exercise will make you sleep like a baby without drugs. Sleep deprivation is one of the risk factors for relapse. Don't let it be one of yours.

"I used to party half the night," says Kim, "and then jack myself up in the morning with huge cups of strong coffee. The drugs in my system combined with caffeine gave me heart palpitations and anxiety attacks. I never want to go that route again."

Relaxation

In today's high-stress world, everyone needs to learn to relax. Those who have previously used drugs or alcohol to promote relaxation will need to learn new techniques. Stress and sleep deprivation cause a body-numbing

Consuming large quantities of caffeinated beverages is an unhealthy way to stay alert; try getting enough sleep instead.

30 | fatigue, but using relaxation techniques will make you feel good.

Biofeedback uses an electronic monitoring device attached to the skin to help you become aware of stress. Eventually you learn to control that stress without the use of the electric monitor. A trained health professional will need to help you with this one.

Progressive muscle relaxation is easy. Sit or lie in a quiet place. Starting with your head, gradually tense various muscles one at a time. Frown, count to seven, relax. Go down the body and repeat the process, from the mouth to the shoulders to the hands, and so on. Tense and relax. Tense and relax until every muscle gets a chance to do both.

Visualization is another easy relaxation technique in which you can create your own mental pictures. In a way, it's like counting sheep to get to sleep. Lie down in a quiet, comfortable place and imagine any scene that seems restful to you. Picture yourself in that place and make the scene last for at least five minutes.

Meditation is similar in some ways to visualization. It is a quiet activity in which breathing is slow, deep, and even. However, in meditation you try to clear your mind of all thoughts. In some forms of meditation, the person repeats a phrase or sound, a "mantra."

Mindfulness is a technique in which you concentrate on the present moment. For example, you are taking a shower in preparation for a date. Instead of thinking about which movie you might go to, you concentrate on the warm water as it courses over your body. Keep your mind on what you are doing rather than on what you will be doing next.

Yoga originated at least 5,000 years ago in India. In the practice of yoga, exercises, body postures, breathing, and meditation help with relaxation and self-control.

T'ai chi, which originated as a Chinese martial art, consists of slow, graceful body movements. You can do it to relieve stress and to encourage healing.

Try these and other relaxation techniques to see what works for you. Don't wait until your vacation to relax. Build some relaxation activities into each day.

Making New Friends

Healthy relationships are an important part of any recovery process. No one says that you have to drop all your former friends, but you will want to avoid your old "using" group. If you are involved in a recovery group such as AA, NA, an aftercare group, or some other therapy group, you are sure to meet new friends who will support you.

Meditation and yoga are great for both mind and body.

Part of your recovery process may involve making amends to those you have hurt because of your drinking or drug use. Do not expect instant forgiveness from everyone. Some people will wait to make sure that you are sincere. A sign in front of a church says "Forgiveness sounds easy until you are the one who has to forgive." All you can do is ask for forgiveness and show by your behavior that you mean what you say.

In the support group that Jim had recently stopped attending, he had made a new friend. Ed, a year older, had continued in the program. One day Ed called Jim and invited him to play tennis. Jim felt honored and got out his racket.

He hadn't played tennis for about a year, and *he had always been pretty bad. Although he wanted to play, the idea of possible failure set off a relapse. Jim didn't meet Ed because he had passed out on the couch.*

When Jim woke up a couple of hours later, a wave of shame and guilt washed over him. He considered letting Ed slip out of his life; after all, he didn't know him that well. But he made himself call. Jim apologized to Ed and asked for another chance. Ed responded, "It's okay, man. I'll see you at group Monday night."

Support Groups

Support groups are an important part of recovery and relapse prevention. Your support group can be an aftercare program; a twelve-step group such as AA, NA, or CA; or some other group organized around the goal of sobriety. Some characteristics of all effective groups include confidentiality (what you say stays in the room), regular meetings, sharing, role modeling, and a common goal.

Some but not all support groups assign a sponsor to a person in recovery. Having a sponsor is a great help in preventing relapse. A sponsor is someone you look up to. This person will have a couple of years of sobriety under his or her belt and will be of the same sex as the recovering addict.

34 This person should be reliable, honest, and able to keep what you say confidential.

Spirituality

You do not have to believe in God or a higher power to achieve sobriety. Programs such as Rational Recovery are set up for people who want to depend on themselves to achieve abstinence. The founder of Rational Recovery, Jack Trimpey, defines "rational recovery" as "the concept of self-recovery from substance addiction through planned abstinence." However, many people find that a strong belief in a supreme being is a tremendous help in avoiding a relapse.

School and Work

The poet Robert Frost said, "By working faithfully eight hours a day, you may eventually get to be a boss and work twelve hours a day." You probably do not want to work twelve hours a day, but it is important to get involved in life. Some people go to school. Others work. Some people go to school and work. Whatever you do, consider that work important. Set achievable goals. When you reach those goals, set more. Be sure to try to find a balance between work and play.

CHAPTER 4

What Causes Relapses?

A relapse is a setback in a person's efforts to change his or her behavior, such as using drugs or alcohol again after a period of abstinence. For some people, a relapse is part of recovery. If you have a relapse, you should not consider it a reason to quit trying. It is not a sign that you have failed. Many people who have had problems with drugs or alcohol in the past will have a relapse, or more than one, in the future. One lapse or slipup does not have to lead to a full-blown return to drug use. A lapse is only one step back. Say to yourself: "One step back; two steps forward." Then get right back to your recovery program.

Are You in Control?
Remember that if you want to stay in control of your life, you cannot let drugs take control of you. To remind yourself

36 how out of control your life felt when you were using drugs, jot down some answers to the following questions:

- What feelings or bad memories did I try to wipe out with the use of drugs or alcohol?
- Whom (besides myself) did I hurt with my drug abuse?
- What things did I do under the influence that I now regret?
- While I was using drugs, how much of life passed me by?
- In what ways did I risk my life (or the lives of others)?

Then, using a scale of 1 to 10, write a number in response to each of the following questions:

- Right now, how close to a 10 is my motivation to stay off drugs and alcohol?
- What number would I assign to my belief that I can do it?
- How close to a 10 do I rate my coping abilities?
- How high do I rate my understanding of the consequences of continued drug use?

Add up your score. If it is close to 40, you are feeling in control and your risk of relapse is low.

Planning for the Possibility of Relapse | *37*

Thinking ahead about possible relapses will not make them happen. In fact, the best way to avoid a relapse is to do some planning in advance. The first step in your plan should be to get a spiral notebook to use as a journal. Start writing in it at least once a day. Write anything that comes to mind related to your recovery process. Later on you can get more specific with statements such as "Did great today" or "Wanted a joint so bad this afternoon I could taste it." This journal will help you to recognize periods of weakness in your recovery process and what triggers them.

Risk Factors

Risk factors are events or situations that can cause a relapse. By identifying these events or situations before they occur, you can gear up for relapse prevention. Risk factors are always out there, and sometimes they are within yourself. Awareness can help you avoid many of them. Try to identify your own possible risk factors in the following categories:

- Troubles in relationships with family and friends.
- Pressures from outside, such as those that come from peers or older

38 siblings. Even the smell of a drug can be a trigger for its use.
- Cravings and urgings to use (pressures from inside).
- Failures, which may make you feel that you are not good enough.
- Problems handling feelings such as anger, depression, guilt, anxiety, or impatience.
- Stress and fatigue.
- Rebellion.
- The desire to "live on the edge."

"In high school and early college," says Josh, "I used everything there was to use except LSD and PCP. One day I got so drunk and so stoned that I had no idea what I was doing. I decided to walk home from a friend's house. The temperature outside was subzero. Later my friends found me almost dead in a snowbank. When I woke up the next morning in a hospital bed, I said to myself, 'Who needs this?' That day I stopped cold turkey.

"I know now that relapse is just a step away. At first I thought that I could go to parties where everyone was drinking and using, but I can't. I found out after several relapses. I have been sober for two years now, and I still can't go to parties. My girlfriend doesn't understand, but she puts up with me. All I have to do is

Moving away from substance abuse can lead to a healthier and happier life, both physically and emotionally.

show her a picture of me when I was using—red eyes, puffy cheeks, and a huge gut. Now I'm fit and firm, I've got my head on straight, and I kind of know where I'm going."

Warning Signs

Warning signs are like little devils perched on your shoulder, shouting messages in your ear: "One hit won't hurt," "Go ahead, it's New Year's Eve," or "You can stop again tomorrow." These tempting voices are warning you that you may be close to relapse.

Warning signs of relapse are often simply subtle changes in feelings and thoughts. Does this mean that every time you find

40 yourself in a bad mood, you are going to have a relapse? No, not if you are prepared. Pay attention to these warning signs and be prepared to strengthen your support system. Warning signs include the following:

- Feeling bored
- Feeling sorry for yourself
- Feeling stressed
- Feeling critical of yourself and others
- Feeling defensive and angry
- Having urges to hang out with users
- Having urges to go to places where you used drugs before
- Rejecting advice
- Denying that you have a problem
- Starting fights
- Lying to yourself and others
- Not discussing feelings
- Isolating yourself from friends and family
- Skipping school
- Stealing
- Getting in trouble with the law

Before his first relapse, Matt had started telling himself that he did not need to go to his recovery group. Everyone else who came had problems that were more serious than his. As a matter of fact, he was getting sick of listening to their stuff. Not only that, but the group took up time he could be spending on profitable activities. *He also talked himself into believing that he could use drugs and alcohol in moderation, which is not an option for an addicted teen.*

Watching for Behavior Patterns

If you have had a previous relapse, or more than one, see if you can find patterns in your behavior that may lead to relapses. Your journal will come in handy here.

Matt figured out that every time he stopped smoking pot or drinking alcohol, two things happened. In the first place, he decided that he could go it alone—without help. He returned to his old haunts and the old friends who hung out there. At the same time, he also began to feel uncomfortable because things were going too well. After talking about these behaviors with his friend Naomi, he began to suspect a pattern and to understand its cause. When he was ten and life was great, his parents announced that they were getting a divorce. At that time, Matt's secure world crumbled. Even back then, he decided that feeling good was not safe. When you felt good, Matt thought, bad things happened. In an effort to dislodge this uncomfortable thought, Matt turned to drugs and alcohol. Recognizing this pattern of behavior and its causes helped Matt to avoid future relapses.

Ask your parents to remove alcohol from your house if doing so will make your recovery easier.

A Fork in the Road

Remember that a relapse is a wrong fork in the road, not necessarily a highway to disaster. A person who is aware of warning signs, watches for risk factors, and identifies patterns that cause relapses is usually able to make a correction before things get serious.

"My parents always said to me, 'Don't drink, don't smoke, don't use drugs,'" Emily reports. "They're giving me this advice while they're drinking martinis in the living room. I'm saying to myself, 'Why not?' I know now that I can't blame them. But I also know that

every time I had a relapse, I would imagine a **43**
picture of them drinking and smoking, and I'd
say to myself, 'If they can do it, why can't I?'
Another risk factor for me was having booze
in the house. After we went to family counsel-
ing, my parents cleaned house and got rid of
the alcohol, which helped."

Parents who stop using drugs and alcohol along with their children are doing their kids a big service. However, teens who are serious about relapse prevention will do what they need to do for themselves—no matter what anyone else does.

CHAPTER 5

Secrets of Relapse Prevention

Social pressure, stress, boredom, negative emotions, cravings, and low self-esteem can all lead to relapse. One of the most common social pressures facing the recovering drug user is the pressure from friends who use. Many young people who stop using drugs or alcohol feel overconfident about their ability to refuse drugs. If you are one of these people, think ahead. Realize that you could be tempted. Other young people lack confidence or feel self-conscious when it comes to saying no. If this person is you, remember that you do not owe anyone an explanation. Practice saying, "No, thanks." If you can, avoid friends who are abusing drugs and find a healthier peer group. Realize that a person bound to you through the common denominator of drug use may not count as a real friend.

Sabrina's old buddies dropped away as she spent more and more time with her music friends. As the lead guitarist in a rock group, she had discovered that a little booze and some drugs helped her write music. In her sober phases, she often wondered what the lyrics meant, but it didn't seem to matter—no one understood the words anyway.

When Sabrina made an effort to get sober, she discovered that associating with her still-using band friends and the venues in which they played triggered her drug and alcohol use. When she finally got serious about recovery, she quit the band. Her old friends fell by the wayside. However, Sabrina had musical talent, and her playing contributed to her positive self-image. She auditioned for a church gospel group and now travels around the state on most weekends. She feels connected to the new people she has met in a way that seems different. She expects some of these new acquaintances to be friends for life.

If the people around you who are using drugs and alcohol are family members, you may not be able to avoid contact with them. If you find yourself in such a situation, increase your attendance at whatever kind of support group helps you. Al-Anon and Alateen help those whose lives have been affected by another person's drinking.

Handling Stress

46

In this frantic, high-tech world there is no way to avoid stress. In fact, some stress is useful; it keeps our brains working to solve problems. When you stop using drugs or alcohol, you may feel out of control because you are not used to dealing with everyday stresses. Remember that when you were using, you were truly out of control. Chemical substances were controlling you. Free of drugs and alcohol, you may wonder why you do not feel more in control. You expected to feel better, not worse.

Finding healthy ways to handle stress will take a while. Be patient and do not give up. Here are a few suggestions for handling stress.

- Be kind to yourself. Sit in a hot tub (if you can find one), take a bubble bath, take a nap, eat something you love, or play your favorite song.
- Get a little exercise.
- Find a sympathetic person to talk to.
- Evaluate your expectations of yourself. Are they too high? Are you trying to do too much? Are you too critical of yourself? Be gentle with yourself; you are making difficult changes. Think of ways to simplify your life. Set attainable goals.

Getting some exercise is a healthy way to manage stress.

- Have some healthy fun.
- When you feel irritable or especially stressed out, try deep breathing. Take a deep breath. Hold it. Let the breath out as you count to seven.
- Say your own version of the Serenity Prayer. In other words, change what you can, accept what you can't change, and try to figure out which is which.

I'm So Bored!

Boredom, the opposite of stress, is another reason for relapse. Boredom is more than a feeling; it's a state of being. In the past, if you have used drugs or alcohol because of boredom, you may be at risk in the future.

48 However, the lifestyle changes you are putting in place—better eating, regular exercise, attendance of support groups, and hard work at school or on the job—will all help keep boredom away.

Consider doing some volunteer work. Helping others almost always makes the helper feel good. You can serve meals at a soup kitchen, have a garage sale and give the profits to your favorite charity, help out at a nursing home, or work for a cause such as saving the whales. If you have never participated in an extracurricular school activity, try one. You will meet new people. You may even develop new skills that will last a lifetime.

If the idea of *planning* your leisure time freaks you out, remember that it may be necessary only in the first stages of recovery. Some people love routine. Doing the same things the same way every day makes them feel secure. Routine bores other people. If you are in the latter category, scramble things up a bit. Eat breakfast at night sometimes. Go to see your grandmother on Saturday instead of Sunday. Bring your mom some roses.

On weekends be sure to keep up your guard. Do not allow yourself too much unstructured time alone. On the other

hand, you cannot schedule every second |
of your life. You need some time to be by yourself. Tell yourself that it is okay to feel bored at times. Being bored is not a sin. You do not need drugs or alcohol to "get over it."

Dealing with Feelings

In recovery, people learn to recognize, accept, and deal with their feelings in healthy ways. Feelings (emotions) make us human. Feelings are neither good nor bad; they just *are*. It's what we do with our emotions that is important. Too often the way we deal with feelings gets us into trouble.

One way that many people, especially those with drug and alcohol problems, deal with feelings is not to deal with them at all. They try to ignore such emotions as anger, fear, sadness, hurt, guilt, loneliness, and even happiness.

"I don't know how I got my name, because happiness was an emotion we didn't express at our house," says Joy. "My parents were both alcoholics. They yelled at each other and at us, and we yelled back at them and at each other. We expressed anger in unhealthy ways. The worst part was that we never learned to express happiness."

Support groups, like this Christian Drug Rehabilitation Service, can help you express your feelings during recovery.

Learning how to express feelings in healthy ways takes hard work and trust. A recovery group is a great place to practice. Listening to others in an environment where no one is blamed may give you the courage to speak up and express your feelings.

Anger is the emotion that gets people with substance abuse problems into the most trouble. Afraid of their own anger, they try to bury it or cover it up with drugs or alcohol. Then, with their inhibitions wiped out, the anger surfaces and explodes like an active volcano. Fallout from the explosion affects everyone in its way and can cause relationship problems for years to come.

No one says that you shouldn't have *51*
angry feelings. Everyone has them. It's how
you handle those feelings that's important.
In his book *Kicking Addictive Habits Once &*
for All, Dennis C. Daley offers a five-step
program to help young people deal with
anger constructively.

1) **Recognize your anger and let yourself feel it.**

How does your anger make your body
feel? Does it give you headaches and stom-
achaches? What does your anger do to your
thoughts? Do you feel like getting even with
someone? How does your anger make you
behave? Does it make you want to increase
your alcohol or drug use? Do you get into fre-
quent arguments or hit people?

2) **Consider all of the possible causes
   of your anger.**

Is your anger justified, or is it irrational?
If it is not really justified, try to change your
thoughts about it. Is your anger directed at
yourself or at your addiction? Is your anger
directed at your parents, or is it directed at
your friends?

3) **Think about the effects of your
   anger on yourself and on others.**

Do you direct your anger inward or do you
project it outward? Do you verbally or physically abuse people because of your anger?

4) Figure out some useful ways to handle your anger.

Go to the person with whom you are angry and express your thoughts in a calm and respectful manner. Talk out your feelings with an objective third party. Work off some of your angry feelings with physical activity. Do not allow your anger to build. Get it out constructively before it becomes destructive to you and others.

5) Evaluate your chosen methods. Why do you think that they might work?

Now that you have a program for handling angry feelings, you can apply this program to problems with other emotions, including fear, sadness or depression, loneliness and emptiness, guilt, and shame.

Dealing with Cravings and Urges

A craving is a desire for immediate gratification. An urge is an intention to engage in an activity to satisfy that craving. If you are in recovery and working to avoid relapses, you will probably experience both cravings and urges.

Expect to experience more cravings in the early stages of your recovery. Use your journal to record, on a scale of 1 to 10, the strength of these urges. Also record the circumstances that led to the craving and your emotional state at the time. Were you happy, sad, angry, bored, or lonely? Later on when you look back in your journal, you will be able to identify the patterns that led to relapses. You will find that physical withdrawal may cause some of your cravings, but psychological factors such as stress can cause more. You may think that a craving will get more and more intense until you give into it. Think of it instead as an urge that subsides when you do not give into it. However, if you do give into your cravings and have a relapse, consider it a one-time event, not a total downslide. Look at a slip as an occurrence that gives you another chance for learning and growth.

Working on Your Self-Esteem

Self-esteem means self-love. No one is born with high self-esteem or low self-esteem. We get it from our backgrounds, from the comments people (our parents, siblings, other relatives, and friends) make about us. If you grew up hearing negative comments and have low self-esteem, it's never too late to change. Every time you say a negative thing to yourself about yourself, change that remark to a positive one. Say: "I'm smart, I am competent, and I can stay free of drugs and alcohol."

Setting realistic goals will help increase your self-esteem and help keep you a

54 drug-free person. Make your goals simple, achievable, and realistic. Say to yourself: "I will exercise for thirty minutes before dinner, and I will not use drugs today."

Self-esteem is a fluid thing. Some days your self-esteem will be higher than on other days. Do not worry. It's normal to have fluctuations. Working on your self-esteem and achieving sobriety are both lifelong processes that take determination and patience.

Reminding Yourself

Jessica makes a "to do" list every day. She uses a black felt-tipped marker to cross off the tasks as she accomplishes them.

Like Jessica, some people want to have a tangible reminder of their goals for the day. If your head is full, writing things down will help.

Some people find it helpful to carry a card with the names of the people they can call upon when they experience the warning signs of relapse. Check with five people to see if they would allow you to put their names and numbers on your card. These people can be family members, supportive friends, a sponsor, or a therapist. Take the "card trick" one step further. Write down on the card exactly what you would say if you had to ask for help. Be prepared.

Glossary

abstinent Being free of drugs and alcohol.

addiction A physical and psychological state in which a person needs a chemical substance to feel normal.

anxiety Uneasiness that something bad could happen.

cardiac arrest Heart stoppage.

compulsive Having to do with irrational urges.

craving A need for immediate gratification; an intense desire for something.

delusion An untrue belief that a person holds on to despite evidence to the contrary.

depressant A chemical substance that causes unnatural sadness.

depression Feelings of sadness and despair that may also involve problems with eating, sleeping, and concentrating; difficulty getting things done; helplessness and hopelessness; and sometimes thoughts of suicide.

flashback A situation in which a person's memory goes back to the

56   drug state—days, weeks, or months after the original experience.

hallucinations   The perceptions of pictures, sounds, odors, and sensations that do not exist.

homicidal thoughts   Thoughts of killing someone else.

intoxication   The mental effects of drug and alcohol use, including confusion or elation.

rehabilitation   Follow-up treatment after detoxification. Sometimes called rehab, rehabilitation helps people learn new ways to live drug-free.

relapse   Going back to using drugs or alcohol after a period of not using.

self-esteem   Self-love; valuing oneself as a person.

susceptible   Readily subject to an influence; vulnerable.

urge   The intention to engage in an activity to satisfy a craving.

withdrawal   Signs and symptoms that occur soon after a person has stopped using drugs or has cut back on heavy drug use. These may include increased pulse rate, tremors, sweating, nausea and vomiting, perspiration, anxiety, agitation, and hallucinations.

Where to Go for Help

In the United States
Al-Anon Family Group Headquarters,
    Inc.
World Service Office (includes Canada)
1600 Corporate Landing Parkway
Virginia Beach, VA 22454-5617
(757) 563-1600
(888) 425-2666
e-mail: wso@alanon.org
Web site: http://www.al-anon.alateen.org

Alcoholics Anonymous
    General Service Office
P.O. Box 459, Grand Central Station
New York, NY 10163
(212) 870-3400
Web site: http://www.aa.org

Cocaine Anonymous
    World Service Office
P.O. Box 2000
Los Angeles, CA 90049-8000
(310) 559-5833
e-mail: publicinfo@ca.org
Web site: http://www.ca.org

58 | The Health Connection
55 West Oak Drive
Hagerstown, MD 21740-7390
(800) 548-8700
e-mail: sales@healthconnection.org
Web site:
   http://www.healthconnection.org

Narcotics Anonymous (NA)
   World Service Office
P.O. Box 9999
Van Nuys, CA 91409
(818) 773-9999
e-mail: Fellowship_Services@na.org
Web site: http://www.narcoticsanony-
   mous.com/

National Clearinghouse for Alcohol and
   Drug Information (NCADI)
P.O. Box 2345
Rockville, MD 20847-2345
(301) 468-2600
(800) 729-6686
Web site: http://www.health.org

National Council on Alcoholism and
   Drug Dependence (NCADD)
12 West 21st Street, Seventh Floor
New York, NY 10010
(212) 206-6770

e-mail: national@NCADD
Web site: http://www.ncadd.org

National Drug Abuse Information
    and Treatment Referral Hotline
    and National Institute on Drug
    Abuse Helpline
12280 Wilkens Avenue
Rockville, MD 20852
(800) 662-HELP
(800) 662-AYUDA (Spanish-speaking)

National Self-Help Clearinghouse
    (NSHC)
25 West 43rd Street, Room 620
New York, NY 10036-7406
(212) 817-1822
Web site: http://www.selfhelpweb.org

Office for Substance Abuse Prevention
Alcohol, Drug Abuse and Mental Health
    Association (ADAMHA)
5515 Security Lane
Rockwell II Building, Suite 900
Rockville, MD 20857
(301) 443-0365
Web site: http://www.samhsa.gov

Women for Sobriety (WFS)
P.O. Box 618

Quakertown, PA 18951
(215) 536-8026
(800) 333-1606
e-mail: NewLife@nni.com
Web site: http://www.mediapulse.com/wfs/

In Canada

Canadian Centre on Substance
   Abuse (CCSA)
75 Albert Street, Suite 300
Ottawa, ON K1P 5E7
(613) 235-4048
Web site: http://www.ccsa.ca/

Kids Help
439 University Avenue, Suite 300
Toronto, ON M5G 1Y8
(416) 586-5437
(416) 586-0100
(800) 668-6868
Web site:
   http://kidshelp.sympatico.ca/index.html

For Further Reading

Chiauzzi, Emil, and Steven K. Liljegren. *Staying Straight: A Relapse Prevention Workbook for Young People.* Holmes Beach, FL: Learning Publications, 1991.

Daley, Dennis C. *Relapse Prevention Workbook: For Recovering Alcoholics and Drug-Dependent Persons.* 2nd ed. Holmes Beach, FL: Learning Publications, 1997.

Daley, Dennis C., and Charles R. Sproule. *Adolescent Relapse Prevention Workbook: A Guide to Staying Off Drugs and Alcohol.* Holmes Beach, FL: Learning Publications, 1991.

Fleming, Martin. *How to Stay Clean and Sober: A Relapse Prevention Guide for Teenagers.* Minneapolis, MN: Johnson Institute, 1991.

Gorski, Terence T. *Relapse Prevention Counseling Workbook: Managing High-Risk Situations.* Independence, MO: Herald House/Independence Press, 1995.

62 | **Challenging Reading**

Daley, Dennis C. *Kicking Addictive Habits Once & for All: A Relapse Prevention Guide.* Lexington, MA: Lexington Books/D. C. Heath and Co., 1991.

Marlatt, Alan G., and Judith Gordon, eds. *Relapse Prevention: Maintenance Strategies in the Treatment of Addictive Behaviors.* New York: The Guilford Press, 1985.

Index

About the Author

Barbara Moe is a mother, a nurse, a social worker, and a writer. She loves working with young people and helping them face challenges.

Photo Credits

Cover photo © Uniphoto; p. 2 © AP Wide World Photos, pp. 6, 10, 15, 18, 24, 29, 39, 42, 47 by Ira Fox; p. 32 by Brian Silak, p. 50 © Corbis.

Design and Layout

Michael J. Caroleo